Luna the Wake-up Cat

Written by Charnan Simon
Illustrated by Benrei Huang

Children's Press®
A Division of Scholastic Inc.
New York • Toronto • London • Auckland • Sydney
Mexico City • New Delhi • Hong Kong
Danbury, Connecticut

For Luna, Lily, Kurt, and Buzz—good cats all!
—C. S.

To Ming-ming and Steve, who wake up their cat every morning.
—B. H.

Reading Consultant

Cecilia Minden-Cupp, PhD
Former Director of the Language and Literacy Program
Harvard Graduate School of Education
Cambridge, Massachusetts

Cover design: The Design Lab
Interior design: Herman Adler

Library of Congress Cataloging-in-Publication Data

Simon, Charnan.
  Luna the Wake-Up Cat / written by Charnan Simon ; illustrated by
Benrei Huang.
      p. cm. — (A rookie reader)
  Summary: A tale of a cat who awakens her owner, enjoys some attention,
then leads the way to breakfast introduces prepositional phrases.
    ISBN-10: 0-531-12087-2 (lib. bdg.)   0-531-12489-4 (pbk.)
    ISBN-13: 978-0-531-12087-3 (lib. bdg.)   978-0-531-12489-5 (pbk.)
  [1. Cats—Fiction. 2. Morning—Fiction. 3. English
language—Prepositions—Fiction.] I. Huang, Benrei, ill. II. Title. III. Series.
  PZ7.S6035Lun 2006
  [E]—dc22   2006006757

CHILDREN'S PRESS, and A ROOKIE READER®, and associated logos
are trademarks and/or registered trademarks of Scholastic Library
Publishing. SCHOLASTIC and associated logos are trademarks and/or
registered trademarks of Scholastic Inc.
1 2 3 4 5 6 7 8 9 10 R 16 15 14 13 12 11 10 09 08 07

Early in the morning,

when the sun first peeks
through my window,

4

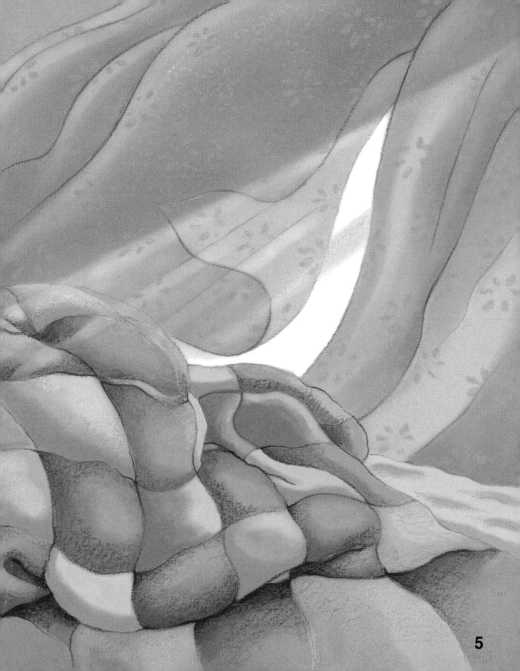

Luna the Wake-up Cat
scratches at my door.

She comes into my room . . .

and jumps on my bed.

Meow! She burrows under my blankets.

She tries to make
herself a cozy nest.

Purrrrrr! She purrs deep in her throat . . .

16

when I tickle her under the chin!

Enough! Luna jumps off the bed.

"Follow me," she seems to say.

She leads me across the hall . . .

down the stairs . . .

and into the bright kitchen
where breakfast is waiting.

Good morning, everyone!

Word List (64 words)

(Words in **bold** are prepositions.)

a	deep	**in**	**off**	throat
across	door	**into**	**on**	**through**
and	**down**	is	peeks	tickle
at	early	jumps	purrrrrr	to
bed	enough	kitchen	purrs	tries
blankets	everyone	leads	room	**under**
breakfast	first	Luna	say	**up**
bright	follow	make	scratches	waiting
burrows	good	me	seems	wake
cat	hall	meow	she	when
chin	her	morning	stairs	where
comes	herself	my	sun	window
cozy	I	nest	the	

About the Author

Charnan Simon lives in Madison, Wisconsin, with her husband and two daughters. She also lives with two cats: the real Luna, who is large and black, and her sister Lily, who is small and grey. Luna and Lily like their breakfasts served promptly.

About the Illustrator

Benrei Huang drew her first children's book in 1988 and has been drawing animals and children ever since. She lives in New York City with her husband and son.